GRAPHIC MYSTERIES

UFOs

ALIEN ABDUCTION AND CLOSE ENCOUNTERS

by Gary Jeffrey

rosen central™

The Rosen Publishing Group, Inc., New York

Published in 2006 by The Rosen Publishing Group, Inc.
29 East 21st Street, New York, NY 10010

First edition, 2006

Designed and produced by
David West Books

Editor: Kate Newport

Photo credits:
Page 4, NOAA; page 5, Michael Knights; page 7 (right), Lee Pettet, (left), George Cairns; page 44 (top) European Association for Astronomy Education; page 44 (bottom), NCAR; page 45, U.S. Air Force photo by Staff Sgt. Aaron D. Allmon I

Library of Congress Cataloging-in-Publication Data

Jeffrey, Gary.
     UFOs : alien abduction and close encounters / by Gary Jeffrey.
     p. cm. – (Graphic mysteries)
     Includes index.
     ISBN 1-4042-0797-X (library binding) – ISBN 1-4042-0808-9 (pbk.) –
     ISBN 1-4042-6265-2 (6 pack)
     1. Unidentified flying objects–Juvenile literature. I. Title. II. Series.

     TL789.2.J44 2005
     001.942–dc22

                              2005017915

Manufactured in China

CONTENTS

WATCH THE SKIES!

People have claimed to have seen mysterious objects in Earth's skies for over 2,000 years. But it was not until the mid-twentieth century that the term "Unidentified Flying Object" was first coined as a label for the phenomenon.

THE FIRST UFO SIGHTING

At 2:50 P.M., Tuesday, June 24, 1947, private pilot Kenneth Arnold was flying east toward Mount Rainier in Washington. Suddenly, nine mysterious objects appeared in the sky in front of him.

They were 30 miles away, at an altitude of 10,000 feet, flying at an estimated speed of 1,200 mph, and weaving in a peculiar motion, "like the tail of a Chinese kite." Arnold described them as "flat like a pie pan and somewhat bat-shaped" and "so shiny they reflected the sun like a mirror."

Mount Rainier in Washington State.

The authorities didn't believe him at first, but his story was soon backed up by other witnesses across the Midwest. Arnold quickly became known in the national press as "The man who saw the men from Mars."

On June 24, 1947, mysterious "saucer-like objects" were spotted over Washington State, Kansas, and Oregon.

Soon after the first eyewitness accounts were published, the idea of the UFO as an alien-controlled flying saucer became fixed in the feverish public imagination.

FLYING SAUCER FEVER!

As Arnold's story spread, other people began to report seeing flying disks all over the United States. It seemed a craze had taken hold.

The U.S. military, however, remained skeptical until two weeks later, when mystery radar targets began showing up on the scopes at their secret bases near Roswell, New Mexico.

The Roswell Incident put UFOs on the world stage, and the U.S. government decided to take action. From 1947 until 1969, the United States Air Force investigated UFO sightings under a series of programs, the most famous of which was called Project Blue Book.

Encouraged by a wave of articles and books that came out in the early 1950s, groups of civilian "ufologists" dedicated themselves to gathering evidence about the sightings. The witnesses they found were often left feeling traumatized and disturbed by their encounters with the strange objects.

CLOSE ENCOUNTERS

Witnessing a UFO in the sky is a Close Encounter of the First Kind. Five years after the first UFO sighting, came Close Encounters of the Second and Third Kind. In these cases, a UFO or its occupants physically interact with their surroundings.

FIRST CONTACTS

On November 20, 1952, in California's Mojave Desert, the first human contact with aliens was recorded. George Adamski, a local hot dog vendor, had been hunting UFOs with six friends when he encountered a strange humanoid figure who stood approximately five feet tall. The alien was friendly and communicated with Adamski using telepathy and sign language.

A diagram of the saucer claimed to have been seen by George Adamski in 1952.

On October 15, 1957, in Minas Gerais, Brazil, farmer Antonio Villas-Boras was working in his fields at night. Out of nowhere, a large, shiny, egg-like object landed in front of his tractor. Startled, he ran, but was caught by four helmeted humanoids in skin-tight gray overalls. He was taken aboard the craft, stripped, washed, and given blood tests.

Following the incident, Villas-Boras was deeply upset and had trouble sleeping. He was examined by a doctor who found that he had been exposed to massive amounts of radiation. These reports hinted at what would come next: a Close Encounter of the Fourth Kind...an alien abduction.

THE FIRST ABDUCTION

On the night of September 19, 1961, Betty and Barney Hill were driving home through New Hampshire. What they described as a "white star" seemed to change into a pancake-shaped UFO. They panicked and sped away.

After this, Betty began to have recurring nightmares about horrible creatures with catlike eyes. They also discovered that during their journey they had "lost" two hours of time.

The couple were then persuaded to undergo hypnosis, which suggested that they had been abducted by aliens and subjected to medical experiments. Many future reports of abductions followed this pattern.

This well-known image of the "gray" alien has evolved from many eyewitness reports gathered over the years.

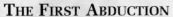

Crop circles and attacks upon cattle are just some of the mysterious occurrences that have been linked to UFOs.

THE ROSWELL INCIDENT

U.S. AIR FORCE MISSILE TESTING BASE, WHITE SANDS, NEW MEXICO, JULY 4, 1947.

FOR THREE DAYS NOW, THE MYSTERY TARGETS HAVE BEEN OVERFLYING OUR BASES AT SPEEDS FAR BEYOND EVEN OUR FASTEST PURSUIT JETS!

DO YOU THINK THEY COULD BE RUSSIANS, MR. KAUFMANN?

THAT'S EXACTLY WHAT THIS GENTLEMAN FROM CIC*, IN WASHINGTON, IS HERE TO FIND OUT!

*COUNTERINTELLIGENCE CORPS

10 P.M. AT THE BACK PORCH OF DAN WILMOT'S HARDWARE STORE, ROSWELL CITY, NEW MEXICO

HONEY, THERE'S A BIG STORM STARTING UP IN THE CANYON. THERE'S GONNA BE A **FREE** FIREWORKS SHOW TONIGHT!

HEY, LOOK! A SHOOTING STAR!

NOW THAT SEEMS STRANGE... AND IT'S HEADING STRAIGHT FOR THE STORM!

MEANWHILE, OVER AT WHITE SANDS...

HOW FAST IS THAT TARGET MOVING?

OVER A THOUSAND MILES AN HOUR. BUT WAIT! SOMETHING'S HAPPENING!

IT'S...PULSATING!

IT'S...GONE!

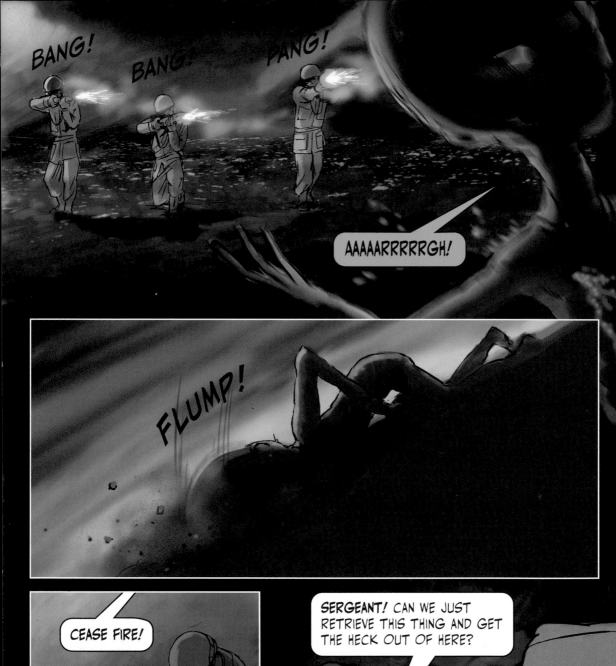

OK, SHOW IS OVER! LET'S GET THIS SITE **CLEARED**!

SIR! VEHICLES ARE APPROACHING FROM THE SOUTH!

HAND ME YOUR FIELD GLASSES.

A FIRE TRUCK AND A PATROL CAR!

TAKE SOME MEN AND REINFORCE THAT PERIMETER. DON'T LET **ANYONE** THROUGH, OK?

MEANWHILE, IN THE CAB OF ROSWELL FIREMAN DAN DWYER'S FIRE TRUCK...

CAN **YOU** SEE ANYTHING YET, DAN?

JUST A BUNCH OF LIGHTS – LOOKS LIKE A DARNED CIRCUS OUT THERE!

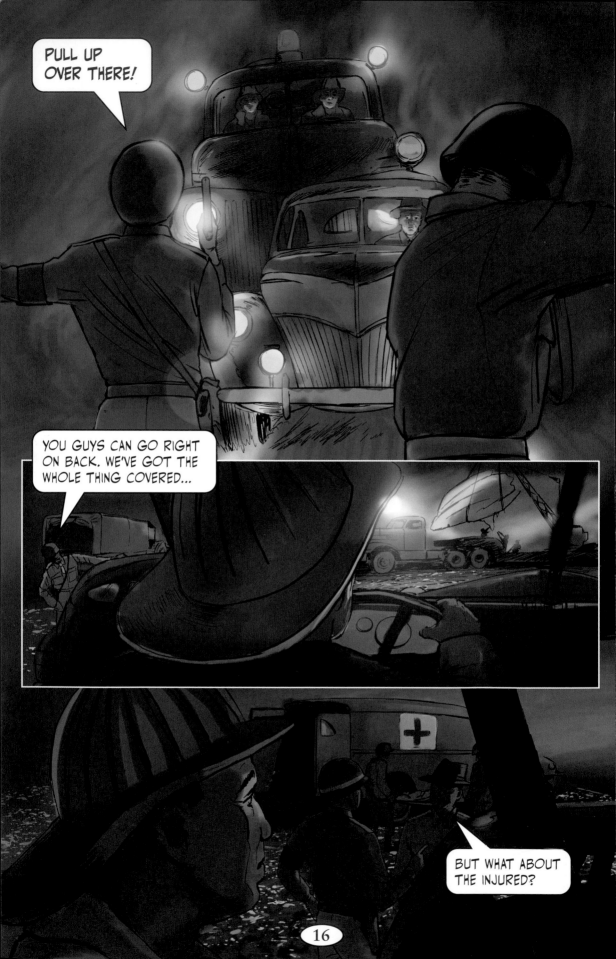

WHAT **ARE** YOU?

YOU'RE NOT FROM THIS WORLD, ARE YOU?

THEN...

DEBRIS EVERYWHERE!

WHAT **IS** THIS STUFF?

METAL?

WE CAN'T LET THE TRAIL LEAD TO CORONA. THEY MUST NOT KNOW WHAT WE FOUND THERE!

SO LET'S **TELL** THE PRESS WE RECOVERED A FLYING DISK OUTSIDE **ROSWELL**...

THAT'S RIGHT! WE NEED TO STOP THIS STORY RIGHT IN ITS TRACKS.

...IT'S A STORY SO FANTASTIC THAT NOBODY WILL TAKE IT SERIOUSLY. MEANWHILE, WE CAN COMPLETELY CLEAR THE CORONA SITE!

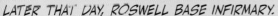

LATER THAT DAY, ROSWELL BASE INFIRMARY.

EXCUSE ME, NURSE! COULD YOU HELP US WITH AN AUTOPSY?

SURE!

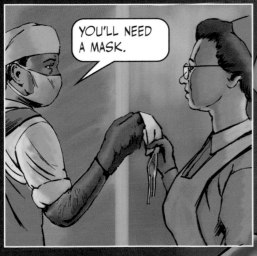

YOU'LL NEED A MASK.

GASP!

WE JUST NEED YOU TO TAKE SOME NOTES...

LATER, IN HANGAR 58.

WE'RE KEEPING MAC BRAZEL AT THE BASE UNTIL THINGS QUIET DOWN.

AT LAST! THE ROSWELL INCIDENT IS OFFICIALLY DEAD!

NOW, WE JUST HAVE TO MAKE SURE IT STAYS THAT WAY.

A FEW DAYS LATER, THE HOUSE OF DAN DWYER, ROSWELL CITY.

BANG! BANG!

SOMEONE'S AT THE DOOR! HONEY, HIDE THAT THING AND WAIT IN THE KITCHEN!

THE ABDUCTION OF TRAVIS WALTON

NOVEMBER 5, 1975, SITGREAVE-APACHE NATIONAL FOREST, ARIZONA. SEVEN WOODCUTTERS ARE RETURNING HOME WHEN THEY ENCOUNTER A STRANGE LIGHT...

TRAVIS – NO! COME BACK!

ZAPP!

GRRRRGH!

?

ANOTHER ROOM!

THE WALLS ARE MELTING INTO STARS AS I WALK TOWARD THE CHAIR!

CLICK!

WHOA! WE'RE MOVING!

THE VARGINHA INVASION

JANUARY 19, 1996, NORTH AMERICAN AEROSPACE DEFENSE COMMAND (NORAD), CHEYENNE MOUNTAIN, COLORADO, USA.

CINDACTA*, THIS IS NORAD, OUR SATELLITES HAVE ALERTED US THAT **MULTIPLE** UNIDENTIFIED TARGETS ARE HEADING YOUR WAY...

THANK YOU, WE WILL NOTIFY OUR FORCES ON THE GROUND.

*BRAZILIAN AIR DEFENSE AND AIR TRAFFIC CONTROL SYSTEM

SOON AFTER, OVER THE TOWN OF VARGINHA IN SOUTH CENTRAL BRAZIL...

LOOK AT THEM ALL!

SOME ARE FLOATING, SOME ARE SPEEDING!

WHAT ARE THEY?

EARLY MORNING, JANUARY 20, SIX MILES OUTSIDE VARGINHA. FARMHAND EURICO RODRIGUES IS WOKEN BY THE FRIGHTENED MOOING OF HIS CATTLE...

ORALINA, COME AND SEE! THERE'S A SUBMARINE FLOATING ABOVE THE PASTURE!

LOOK! IT'S SMOKING! YOU THINK MAYBE IT'S IN TROUBLE?

8 A.M., VARGINHA FIRE DEPARTMENT.

GUYS, GET YOUR GEAR! A STRANGE ANIMAL HAS BEEN REPORTED LOOSE NEAR THE WOODS AT JARDIM ANDERE.

WHEN THEY ARRIVE...

HEY, LOOK! THE ARMY'S HERE ALREADY.

BRRRRZZZZZZZT!

LEAVE IT! RUN!

RUN!

LATER, THE GIRLS RETURN WITH HELP BUT FIND THE CREATURE GONE.

LOOK, THE GRASS IS FLATTENED HERE!

AND IT STINKS LIKE AMMONIA!

THE ONLY THING TO DO IS REPORT IT!

A FEW HOURS LATER...

NOTHING, NO TRACE. BUT THOSE GIRLS SEEMED PRETTY SCARED TO ME.

MARCO, IT'S A HOAX! THAT'S WHY THEY SENT TWO MILITARY POLICEMEN INSTEAD OF A PLATOON!

WHAT ON EARTH?

DOC, CAN YOU TELL ME HOW THIS CREATURE DIED?

I'M NOT SURE. I'VE NEVER SEEN ANYTHING LIKE THIS – I MEAN, LOOK AT ITS TONGUE...!

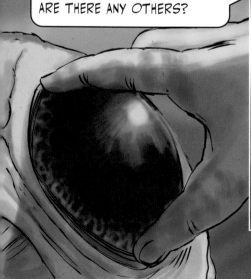

...AND THESE EYES! WHERE DID THE CREATURE COME FROM? ARE THERE ANY OTHERS?

YES, BUT THEY ARE ALL SAFELY LOCKED AWAY...

UFOs – FACT OR FICTION?

Are witnesses to UFOs seeing actual alien craft in the skies, or is there another explanation? Have people really encountered and been abducted by creatures from other planets, or are they imagining it?

The light from the planet Venus is often mistaken for a UFO.

MISTAKEN IDENTITY

The 1947 Kenneth Arnold sighting that started it all has since been explained as a formation of white pelicans bathed in light reflected from snow-covered mountains.

Many alleged UFO sightings are actually the planet Venus and shooting stars (meteor events). In addition, orbiting debris from old space missions can burn up in Earth's atmosphere, causing fires in the sky. A famous incident at a U.S. airbase near Rendlesham Forest, in England, was explained as light from a local lighthouse streaming through the trees.

Lenticular (lens shaped) clouds can resemble giant flying saucers.

NATURAL PHENOMENA

Strange cloud formations (left), ball lightning, electromagnetic emissions from rocks, and temperature shifts that cause false radar emissions, have all been mistaken over the years for signs of extraterrestrial activity on Earth.

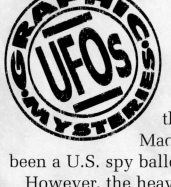

GOVERNMENT SECRECY

In 1994, the United States Air Force investigation into the Roswell incident established that the debris discovered on Mac Brazel's ranch in 1947 had been a U.S. spy balloon and not an alien spacecraft.

However, the heavy-handed tactics of the authorities in suppressing the true story planted a seed of distrust with the public. Over the years, this distrust grew into outright paranoia about the government's secret involvement with UFOs. The well-known conspiracy theories involving captured spacecraft, experiments on aliens, and the use of alien technology have their roots in the cover-up at Roswell in 1947.

In the 1990s, people began seeing black diamond-shaped UFOs. Could some of these sightings have been of the then top secret Stealth fighter undergoing test flights?

RECOVERED MEMORIES

A shared feature of many alien abduction cases is memory loss by the abductee after the event. Starting with the Hills, nearly all victims have needed to have their experiences recovered under hypnosis. This has led skeptics to question the reliability of their testimonies. Travis Walton's case was further weakened by his acceptance of a $5,000 payment from a tabloid newspaper for supplying evidence of extraterrestrial activity.

At the present time, while some objects in the sky may be unidentified, they are not likely to be craft from outer space.

GLOSSARY

abduction When a person is taken somewhere illegally and against his or her will.

affirmative An expression used to confirm the previous statement or command.

autopsy A medical examination of a body carried out after death.

canyon A deep narrow valley with very steep sides.

cargo The contents of a plane, ship, train, or truck.

civilian An ordinary citizen who is not a member of any of the armed services.

debris The remains of something, such as an aircraft, that has broken apart or been destroyed.

"diabos" Portuguese word for the devil.

extraterrestrial A being that originates, occurs, or exists outside of Earth's atmosphere.

generator A machine that provides electrical energy.

hangar An enclosed area for repairing and storing aircraft.

hoax A trick that makes people believe in the reality of something that is fake.

infirmary Another word for a hospital.

intelligence Information or evidence concerning a possible enemy.

"Meu Deus" Portuguese saying used to express surprise. In English it means "My God!"

mortuary A building or room where dead bodies are kept until burial or cremation.

mutant Living thing that is either physically or genetically different from other members of its species.

perimeter A boundary that marks off and protects an area.

phenomenon An unusual event, observed through one's senses.

platoon A subdivision of a military unit or company.

pupil The opening in the middle of an eye that appears to be black.

radar A machine that detects objects and their positions using radio waves.

radiation Energy transmitted through waves.

retrieve To find and bring something back.

ruskie A negative nickname for Russians.

satellite Communications device that orbits Earth.

sentry A soldier who guards a particular post.

stench A strong, unpleasant smell.

suppress To put something down with force or to keep it secret.

telepathy A wordless exchange of thoughts.

unidentified Unable to be labeled or classified.

FOR MORE INFORMATION

ORGANIZATIONS

International UFO Museum and Research Center
Roswell, New Mexico
114 North Main Street
Roswell, NM 88203
(505) 625-9495
Web site: http://www.iufomrc.com

Museum of New Mexico
107 West Palace Avenue
Santa Fe, NM 87501
(505) 982-6366
Web site: http://www.museumfoundation.org

FOR FURTHER READING

Levy, J. *Guide to the Unexplained* (KISS). London, England: DK, 2002.

Picknett, Lynn. *The Mammoth Book of UFOs.* London, England: Constable Publishers, 2001.

Rosenberg, Aaron. *UFOs* (Unsolved Mysteries). New York: The Rosen Publishing Group, Inc., 2002.

Tiger, Caroline. *The UFO Hunter's Handbook.* New York: Price Stern Sloan, 2001.

Young, Caroline. *UFOs* (Usborne Hotshots). London, England: Usborne, 1997.

INDEX

Web Sites

Due to the changing nature of Internet links, the Rosen Publishing Group, Inc., has developed an online list of Web sites related to the subject of this book. This site is updated regularly. Please use this link to access the list:

http://www.rosenlinks.com/grmy/ufos